Managers as Leaders
Managers Organise, Leaders Deliver

Copyright © George P Boulden

All Rights Reserved

No part of this book may be reproduced in any form, by photocopying or by any electronic or mechanical means, Including information storage or retrieval systems, without permission in writing from both the copyright owner and the publisher of this book.

ISBN 978-0-9560822-2-0

First Published October 2008

ALA INTERNATIONAL PUBLISHING

Lutterworth, England - alapub@ala-international.com

Email – george.boulden@ala-international.com

Web - www.ala-international.com

Printed in Great Britain by ALA International Publishing

Ed. 3   November 2023

Content

....	1
Contrnt	3
Synopsis	6
Acknowledgements	7
What is Management	9
Leadership	14
The Leadership Equation	20
Authority	**21**
Leadership Style	**25**
Delivery - Communicating what needs to be done	**28**
Leading your Team	31
Using the - The 'Four Factor' Model	37
Analysing the results	**42**
Read the 'meta' Message	**46**
Action - Decide what to do	**47**
Implement	**48**
Review and reinforce	**49**
The Way Ahead	51
Leadership Skills – Self Assessment Check List	**51**
Further Reading	55

Synopsis

Management is a process; leadership is a skill. Management is concerned with creating the message; leadership is about delivering the message. Managers are appointed, normally because they are seen to be 'good at the job'; leaders are the people chosen by the people who do the job.

To be effective in a management position the holder needs to both be able to plan and organise what needs to be done and the leadership skills to deliver it. This book explains both the management and leadership processes and shows how they can be used together.

Acknowledgements

I would like to begin by acknowledging the great debt of gratitude I owe to Professor Reginald (Reg) Revans, the founder of the Action Learning movement. We met in 1974 when he was planning his first Action Learning programme in GEC. At the time of our first meeting, I had recently transferred from line management into a management development role. I was very aware that mature managers did not respond well to 'teaching' and was searching for ways of creating learning opportunities. Over lunch Reg shared his ideas with me and I was sold; thirty-five years later I am still a convinced action learner. He introduced me to Alan Lawlor who pioneered Own Job Action Learning in the West Midlands and the three of us created Action Learning Associates (ALA) Intentional in 1980 to promote the application of Action Learning. My relationship with Reg continued until his death in 2003.

I would also like to acknowledge my good friends Malcolm Farnsworth, John Cooper and Professor Steve Iman of Cal Poly Pomona CA.

Malcolm, who as Principal of the Marconi Staff Development Centre in Chelmsford, gave me the chance of a new career in management development which I have pursued for a very stimulating thirty-five years.

John, who I worked with at Dunchurch Staff College, is a natural 'action learner' as anyone who has used or experienced the marvellous business simulations he created will testify and generous to a fault with everything he did. For me John is one of the unsung heroes of Action Learning and deserves to be recognised as such.

Steve for his encouragement and enormous contribution to the publication of the book; without Steve's guiding hand it would probably never have seen the light of day'

Finally I would like to thank the many hundreds of participants and clients from around the globe who I have learned with and from over the years. It has been a great privilege to know you, thank you all.

George P Boulden - May 2015

What is Management

Management is concerned with obtaining and controlling resources to achieve given objectives. Effective mangers:-

Recognise what needs to be done **(the task, goal, or objective)**
Specify and obtain the **resources** to do it
Decide how to manage those resources to get the task done **(process to follow)**
Direct and control the use of those resources, *in action*, to achieve the desired result(s) **(skill and courage to follow the process)**

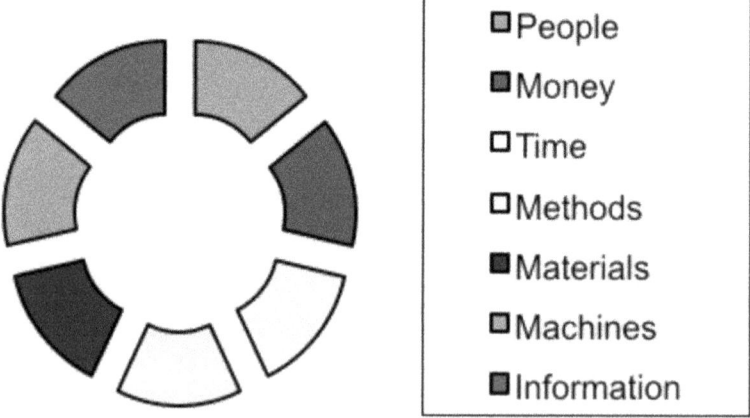

PHYSICAL RESOURCES

- People
- Money
- Time
- Methods
- Materials
- Machines
- Information

In addition to these 'physical' resources managers must also create and control *The Working Environment*. This is the climate in which the work takes place; the 'style' of doing things. It embraces such 'soft' concepts as:
Communication & Information flows
Leadership

Motivation
Team working
Decision making style
Politics, power, and influence

Communication & Information flows are not usually listed as one of the classic management resources. But where rates of change and technological development are high the ability to control information flows can be critical to an organisation's success; it therefore merits being seen as a key resource.

Managers use the **"managing process"** to manage their resources to that the objective or task is achieved in an efficient manner. Following this process ensures that the stages that must be gone through to achieve a given goal are undertaken in a disciplined and systematic way.

Set Objectives	*'what' specifically is the objective (for each of the resources - People, Money, Methods, Machines, Materials, Time, Information flows.)*
Decide Policy	*'how', in general terms, should the objective be achieved.*
Plan	*for each resource (Time, Money, People etc.) what steps are necessary to achieve the goal.*
Organise	*bring together the resources required for the plan.*
Direct	*implement the plan.*
Control	*measure, monitor actual results; compare against the plan; re-plan as necessary.*

Broadly speaking the process is carried out at three different levels within organisations *and is applied to each resource in turn - money, machines etc.*:

1. Senior managers are responsible for creating the Vision – the where the organisation going Goals – 'what' we need to get there and the Strategy – the 'how.'
2. Middle managers take the top-level goals and strategies and develop policies and plans for their implementation using the managing process to communicate with their staff.
3. First line managers and supervisors take the policies and plans set by their functional heads and (again using the *managing process*) and break them down into work tasks which they then manage their people to achieve.

This can be thought of like a mountain, which has a sparse population at its summit but has a great deal of 'hustle and bustle' in the villages and towns on the lower slopes. From the top of the 'management mountain' senior managers have a view of the 'big picture' but often have little idea of the hive of activity that is taking place below them: junior managers at the bottom of the 'mountain' have a good understanding of what needs to be done and the 'here and now' decisions that are needed but are limited in how far they can see. Middle managers see something from both above and below and have the task of translating and co-ordinating the strategies from above into deliverables at the operating level and ensuring compliance. This ensures that the 'doers' at the lower levels have explicit information about what needs doing, the desired quality of the activity, the times scales and costs that can be incurred. Thus ensuring that they focus their efforts in the right direction. Below is a simplified example of the cascading management process in action for some of the issues associated with the People Resource:-

PROCESS	People
	TOP LEVEL

Objectives	Efficient utilisation of all assets
Policy	To optimise performance To treat people with respect and dignity To help people reach their full potential To ensure that people are properly trained to do their jobs
Plan	Role descriptions for all employees exist & current Annual performance appraisals for all employees completed by end April each year Five days training per year per employee

	MIDDLE LEVEL
Objectives	Efficient utilisation of all employees in line with the framework set by senior managers
Policy	Each manager/supervisor to have responsibility for applying the senior management plan to his/her area with overall compliance to be monitored on a monthly basis by department heads.
Plan	Review role descriptions each quarter Ensure all managers are trained in appraisal interviewing by March 1st Complete annual appraisals by April 10th Department head to review 4 appraisal forms per section as a quality check by April 15th Identify 5 days training for individual employees by April 10th Department head to review training plans each quarter

	JUNIOR LEVEL
Objectives	Efficient utilisation of all employees in line with the framework set by senior and middle managers
Policy	First line managers and supervisor to have responsibility for applying the middle management plan in their work area.
Plan	Check that role description is still current by talking with job holders once a quarter Delegate work and monitor performance Schedule appraisal interviews to be completed by April 10th Schedule interviews to ensure that training plans are complete by April 10th Monitor implementation of training plans by holding monthly meetings with each employee

This is management; a process of organising planning and controlling. However, just cascading even 'good' information down the organisational pyramid is not enough; telling people what to do does not engage their hearts and minds. To be 'motivated' to work people need to feel that what they are doing has value; that the organisation wants them to 'bring their brains to work'. This is when managers become leaders. They take the 'work package' they have been given through the 'management process' and re-package it into a form that will motivate their people to succeed and provide the environment to make this happen; this is leadership.

Leadership

Leadership is *the ability of one individual to meet the needs of others who are either seeking someone to lead them or who, for whatever reason, are willing to follow.* Successful leaders are people with vision, they know what they want, they understand how to get it, what has to be done, and they have the courage of their convictions.

There is no one successful style of leadership. No one type of effective leader for all situations. It's horses for courses; different leaders are required at different times and in different circumstances. In the preparation stage of a new project for example, the leader must be able to "see" the goal and help the team clarify its understanding of what it is trying to achieve. In the development stage they must be able to lead the team through process of producing an effective plan. In the launch phase he/she must be able to delegate, to set performance targets. During implementation he must be able to monitor and control.

The early work on leadership focused on the trait theory. This took the view that great leaders are born not made. It suggested that great leaders have common characteristics, things like physical size, charisma, charm, a good education, a penchant for hard work etc. This is clearly not the case. Many of the great leaders of history were small in stature, often cruel; many had little education and a penchant for manipulation rather than hard work.

The 'style' theorists followed. Their approach takes the view that style, the way the leader leads, is the key to success. Douglas McGregor led the way with his theory X theory Y. His work was complemented by the Tannenbaum & Schmidt Leadership Continuum. They identified five different styles of leadership, each having a part to play in the successful leadership of groups. The basis of this was the belief that managers would obtain better results from their people if they recognised people's needs change depending on the circumstance's and choose the most appropriate style to meet those needs. Thus managers wanting to increase productivity, recognising that the best approach (McGregor) would be through greater worker involvement would choose a 'participative' (Tannenbaum & Schmidt) style of managing.

These theories were combined into a practical model by Rensis Likert in his System 4 approach. His work showed clearly that whilst autocracy produced good short-term results, the best results over time were produced by workers who were involved in the work through the use of a participative style. B.F. Skinner's work on positive reinforcement (see People Express) also falls into this style category.

The 'style' theorists were followed by a group who looked at leadership in the context of management and aimed to make managers into more effective leaders. These approaches offer a 'desirable style' model; a 'best way' leadership methodology and provide training in its application. John Adair's' Action Centred Leadership model, focuses on the manager's responsibility for providing balanced leadership within the work group. Creating and maintaining the balance between the needs of TASK, the needs of GROUP, and the needs of the INDIVIDUAL.

Blake and Moulton introduced the concept of 'profiling' using a repertory grid to measure management behaviour against a 'best practice' model. Their approach assumes managerial leadership effectiveness can be increased through training managers to balance their concerns for the needs of production with the needs of people. Applying their theory in practice means starting with an agreement on the organisation's 'desired' leadership style. Managers are then profiled to assess their current style and where this does not match the desired profile they are trained to utilise the desired style. Bill Redan's 3D Theory had a similar objective. It links the task, with people and adds the dimension of effectiveness; the results the manager achieves.

More recently there have been the 'situational' theorists. These see the effective leader as someone who is adaptable and who can reflect the 'needs of the situation'. They link task achievement with the leader ability to respond to the changing needs of the situation. The leading exponents in this area include such people as F.E. Fielder whose theory of effective leadership links the reality of the current situation with the leaders chosen actions and style (also see Hersy & Blanchard - Situational Leadership. They suggest that effective leaders flex their leadership interventions to 'provide the leadership followers need' in different situations. When an employee is performing well the leader focuses on reward and recognition. When employees have problems the situational leader provides direction etc.

Whilst each theory presents an interpretation of what makes effective leaders, taken together they tell us that there is no 'right' approach to leadership, or right leader'. The people choose their leaders by accepting their authority. It is this acceptance of authority that 'allows' an individual to lead, which means that the leader, to be accepted as a leader, must meet the needs of the follower; effective leaders recognise the needs of others and provide direction that others are willing to follow.

In the natural world people change their leaders' changes depending on the circumstances. Anyone can be and is accepted as a leader when their skills, knowledge or beliefs are appropriate to what the people need. If the goal is to maximise effectiveness, the people will follow the person or people who they believe can help them to achieve this goal. If it's negotiating a pay rise they will follow those who they believe are most likely to be successful at this and so on.

So how can managers become effective leaders? We believe that the key to being an effective leader lies in being able to create the conditions for success.

Organisational effectiveness starts at the top. Senior managers must agree what they want to achieve, then they must decide how they will utilise the resources, including their people to achieve it. Traditionally the 'how' has been through direction, telling people what to do. It is clear that this is no longer effective. Today there is a need to balance task (what) and process (how) in a way which involves people, thus securing ownership and commitment. The 'great man' approach focuses on task, and certainly appears to work in a crisis. The 'great man' knows what he wants; his people just have to do what they are told. But this approach is only successful if the 'great man' is right and if the people are willing to do what they are told. There is an increasing level of understanding in organisations today however that:

1. there is little chance today of finding 'great men'. Those who have the answers to the organisations problems

2. those who do exist may solve the immediate problems, but their utility is short lived; they inevitably fail and the disruption they create in the process usually outweighs any short-term gains. Note. We only need to look at the 'great leaders' of the Finance sector in in recent years to see the truth of this.

The effective leaders of today, the 'great men' are the 'process' leaders, those who know how to empower people. This trend can be seen in the corporate leadership as found in 'World Class' organisations. These focus on teaming and empowerment, linking the whole organisation together through a network of interlocking teams all with complimentary objects, all performance managed to achieve the final goal.

My observations, after over fifty years of working for and with organisations around the world, lead me to the conclusion that the really effective leaders of today are process orientated, they:

1. Have a vision of the future which encapsulates the needs of the potential followers. Yesterday it was what, today it is how.

2. Know how to get there - Yesterday it was 'follow me', today it is order and process. See Michael Maccoby and his concept of organisational competency.

3. They have the courage to travel, and they understand the role of organisational culture in organisational performance and create effective operational climates - those which reward the desired leadership style lower down.

They know what they want to achieve and recognise that they cannot do it on their own. The ownership and commitment of others is integral to their own success and that an understanding of the needs of their followers is key to this. They analyse these against their own goal(s) and decide what to do. Once this decision has been made they identify the most appropriate authority base and style. They analyse the culture to identify what is acceptable, and they use this information to develop leadership strategies. They then plan and deliver these, reviewing and correcting as they go along.

This means that in practice organisations need two levels of leadership. They need corporate leadership provided by the top team which sets out what should be achieved and the game plan; how it will be done. These 'rules of engagement' are then used to manage the organisation. They create the operational climate in which managers and others lead their respective works teams. Clearly the senior management team are both originators and players in this game. Having made the rules they must live by them themselves, and ensure that all managers in the organisation do the same

Effective leadership starts at the top; as at the top so at the bottom. If the top is confused, aggressive, uncaring, unprincipled et al, the bottom will be the same. Senior managers determine the climate in which their people live and work through the operational climate they create. Thus senior managers dictate the leadership style and behaviours of those below them. They either do this positively, through deciding how managers will manage and setting up the managing systems to ensure this happens, or negatively, taking a laissez faire attitude to the 'how' part of the managing process, leaving junior managers to decide for themselves the most appropriate style.

The objective of any organisation wishing to survive in this competitive world must be flexibility; the ability to 'ride the waves of change'. This means not only being able to satisfy todays needs but also to being able to forecast the needs of tomorrow and adjust to the changing characteristics of the wave before it breaks. Flexible leadership is the key to survival.

The Leadership Equation

Management is the process of structuring and controlling the achievement of tasks. It starts with objectives and finishes when the task is complete. In practice leadership is an integral part of management and is concerned with the way managers carry out the interpersonal aspects of their roles; the way they interact with others to get things done. All managers are leaders in the sense that they have to get things done through others. Some managers are both good managers, they can organise and effective leaders, they can interface with their people both as groups and individuals to get things done. Some are good at the 'process', they can conceptualise and plan but can't communicate their ideas in a way which motivates people; so they are poor leaders. Some managers are good leaders, they have vision and Charisma, that carries people with them, but they cannot organise; so they are poor managers.

Organisations need people in management positions who are both capable managers and effective leaders. They need capable management to organise the achievement of the goals and effective leaders, people who can communicate the message, to ensure the successful realisation of those goals.

Our experience suggests that the most effective approach to the task of leadership is through the concept of **follower-ship**. This means understanding the needs of the people you would like to lead and their likely response to what you want them to do. Then using this assessment to identify common ground and potential problems and being prepared to handle these. Follower-ship is the most important factor in the leadership equation. Without followers there is no one to lead. It is the follower, not the leader, who has the power. Leaders can only exercise that power which the followers are willing to give them. If subordinates do not recognise the manager's authority, either through direct challenge or by ignoring what they say, he/she has no authority. All groups have the power to either accept authority, thus recognising the leader, or by withdrawing their acceptance, to reject the leader.

We said earlier that an understanding of people's leadership needs is the key to the effective management of people. This truth is equally important for all levels of management, for we are all both leader and follower at different times. In essence, it is the need to follow which initiates our acceptance of leadership; the need for someone who will guide us in areas where we are unsure. It is the ability to 'tune in' to this need which is the essence of effective leadership.

There are three ingredients to the leadership equation:-

o   Authority - Understanding the leadership needs that people have and the authority available to the leader

o   Style - Choosing the most appropriate style for the situation

o   Delivery (Communication) - Having the interpersonal skills to do it

Authority

People's acceptance of someone else's 'right' to lead is basic to the leadership process. This acceptance of authority is determined by the 'authority bases' built into our value systems. These are the responses to authority which are programmed into human beings in childhood. They are the main tools used to control people's behaviour in later life and are the basic means by which one human being exerts authority over another. They are the subconscious forces which make individuals respond to the demands of others who they see as having the psychological right to exercise authority over them. There are four main authority bases involved in managing people at work:-

LEADERSHIP AND AUTHORITY - AUTHORITY BASES/NEEDS

Sapiential authority - The authority of knowledge

We are brought up to recognise the value of people who 'know' more than we do and be prepared to learn from them. Therefore, if an organisation appoints the best engineer in the team to be the supervisor, he/she brings to the job their knowledge authority base. This means that as far as the technical aspects of the job are concerned, people in the section, recognising that he/she knows more than they do will respond to their leadership in technical things.

Charismatic authority - The authority of personality

There have always been people in the world who have stronger personalities than the majority. When 'ordinary' individuals meet such people in a group situation, they tend to respond to their leadership. `Free choice' leadership situations are decided on the basis of charismatic authority. Politicians, trades union leaders, local councillors for example, are elected because of their charisma, they can influence people. This authority base is essential for satisfying group needs and team building.

Organisational authority - The authority to organise and control others

This authority base is in two parts 'organisational' and 'controlling' authority.

Organisational authority reflects the leader as an organiser; someone who knows how to do things like organising meetings, managing projects, solving problems, finding resources, making presentations et al. By providing such structures leaders enable their people to work effectively together and are automatically seen as the leader because they know how.

Controlling authority is concerned with keeping order, monitoring performance, disciplining etc. Positively used it focuses on respect. Negatively employed it uses fear. It represents the authority of the Father figure, the schoolmaster, the policeman, the vicar, etc. The negative aspects of structural authority should be used sparingly or they `wear' out. There is a limit to the number of times someone can be threatened. Above that limit they are no longer afraid. Good managers use the organisational aspect of structural authority to monitor and control thus they rarely need to use the disciplinary part.

Moral authority - The authority of being older and wiser.

We are brought up to respect those in our community who are older and wiser and to accept what these people say, particularly on personal issues. Because this authority base is a function of wisdom/age, it is not possible to exercise it without a few grey hairs. Therefore, the young person who is promoted to a management position may well find that although he/she is technically able and has the structural authority of the organisation to back them, they may still find it difficult to be seen as credible in dealing with personal issues especially with older members of the team.

As was said earlier, in a free situation leaders are chosen by followers because they satisfy certain needs. This means they are naturally equipped with the relevant 'authority'. Managers on the other hand are chosen by their bosses for a variety of reasons, none of which necessarily includes their ability to lead others. This means that those who do not have natural leadership skills need to learn to lead if they are to be successful.

The following model outlines the role of each authority base in the managing function. The manager/leaders task is to keep the four areas in balance. If for any reason one goes out of balance, the overall job suffers. To be an effective leader the manager must recognise these areas of `need' and provide leadership in them. Where a manager is not capable of satisfying one or more aspects, for whatever reason, he / she can still be effective by creating a situation where someone else leads, using the manager's authority. The technical manager, whose `sapiential' knowledge on a specific issue is weak, can work effectively by using his / her position to 'link' those in the team with this knowledge with those who need it. Managers who are not very `charismatic' can alleviate this weakness by involving other members of the team in leading meetings and social situations. The manager who is not old enough to be seen as `older and wiser' can always route this type personal problem through someone who is. The manager who can't organise can always delegate.

The secret of effective leadership lies in recognising these needs and ensuring that they are met; if not directly by you, by someone who you delegate to it; in this way the leader retains their authority.

Note. The one task that a leader cannot delegate is 'structural' authority; only the manager can be responsible for discipline. People expect to be disciplined if they do something which is not acceptable and they expect their manager to do it.

Leadership Style

This is the style leaders employ in handling the relationship between themselves and their people. If the style meets the follower's expectations and needs, the end result will be successful for both; if it doesn't, it will be successful for neither. Therefore the manager's choice of style is fundamental to the success of the managing process. There are a range of styles to choose from. To be successful the choice must reflect the:-

* type of decision
* authority base(s) available
* needs of the followers

The following continuum developed by Tannenbaum and Schmidt (ibid) shows the range of styles available.

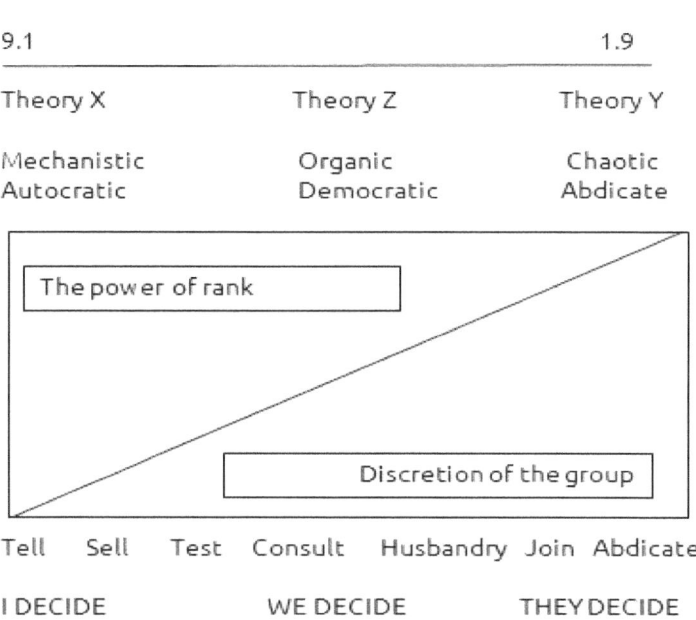

Recognising the Style in Action

Tell : Direct instruction usually prefixed, I want x by Friday. Can be modified to, could you, would you, etc. but means the same. Used when giving a direct order. Decisions I must make because of - urgency time, cost, responsibility, my overall knowledge of the situation etc.

Sell: The originator has already decided what he / she wants done. This behaviour is designed to make the other party more compliant. It's a trading situation; used when the originator is willing to trade to gain commitment.

Test: The leader presents an issue or proposed change to the team and seeks their views on it. Used when the decision maker wants to ascertain likely responses to a proposed course of action before 'going public'

Consult: Like 'test' but no decision made by the originator until all parties have been consulted, the originator then makes the decision. Used for decisions to which the group can/would expect to contribute.

Husbandry: The leader decides the broad objectives but realises that the group has the necessary skills/ability to do the job effectively without him/her, so passes the issue with specification to the group. The observable symptoms are that group work conscientiously towards goal; the manager provides all necessary resources. The leader is seen as supportive and available when required. This style is used when delegating and to develop subordinates.

Join : The leader uses the group to reach decision. Used when all are involved and will have to live with the end result.

Abdicate : The leader presents problem then opts out and leaves decisions to group. Used when problem really belongs to someone else like organising the end of year team party for example.

Note : Our research suggests that Tell, Sell and Test are the styles most commonly used by managers as they are seen to be those which are identified with the management role. Consulting is much less common and is usually considered to denote weakness on the part of those who employ it. Abdication is the favoured alternative to the directing style for autocratic managers.

Delivery - Communicating what needs to be done

Every decision a manager makes needs to be implemented. The manager's ability to get others to do what he/she wants is dependent on their ability to communicate. This means at the one extreme being able to communicate formally, present the plan to whole work force, say 1000 people. It also means being able to argue a plan through a peer group meeting and at the other extreme being able to sit down one on one and convince someone who is highly sceptical that the idea is worthwhile.

This is a complex process involving as it does the:

1. manager/leader, who clearly knows what he/she wants and sees further discussion as largely a waste of time

2. receiver, who may or may not know what is going on and who probably suspects a hidden agenda

3. organisation, which has a culturally acceptable way of doing things which both manager and managed are expected to follow

Traditionally, successful managers were 'task' people. They knew what they were doing, and told others how to get things done. The way such people communicated their decisions was typically authoritarian (parent/child); those who worked with them either followed or left. The conditions today are different. Knowledge is no longer the prerogative of management and toady's people are increasing less willing to respond to being told what to do, they expect to be involved. This means not only communicating ideas differently, but also being willing to debate them in order to gain commitment. This need is changing the whole concept of decision making in organisations. There is little point in managers making decisions that may well be changed through discussion with their people. The approach today is for managers to present the situations to their people and to decide together. In this changing situation managers who will be leaders in the future must have much better 'communication' skills has been required in the past. They need to adopt the styles relevant to their situation and need to deliver them in the appropriate way.

Organisations are also changing their requirements in terms of the managing style. Successful organisations, the world class players, provide guidance on the 'style of management they want their managers to use. Today they don't want 'great man' leaders, people who are the centre of everything, who when they leave take their successes/failures with them. They want consistency. They want managers who create successful organisations, not personality cults. They need managers who can survive and flourish in conditions of rapid change. Managers who are team players empowering their people through managing the process not the task. Setting objectives, agreeing performance targets, monitoring and controlling performance to ensure the organisation's goals are achieved. They want mangers who will involve employees at all levels in problem solving and decision making, enabling them to maximise their contribution to the organisations' goals. This requires different characteristics; an open and participative style of leadership.

Leadership starts at the point when the manager, having decided on a course of action, must put this into practice. The first consideration is what `authority bases' are available. If he knows the answers he/she can use sapiential authority. If not charismatic linked with organisational authority, getting the group together and asking them to solve the problem may be the most appropriate approach. Having chosen the authority base the follower is most likely to be receptive to the leader must then choose the `style'. If he / she knows the answer it may be appropriate to tell the follower(s) what to do. If not consultation, involving the follower(s) in deciding what should be done may be the most appropriate approach.

Whatever the situation, the skill of the effective leader is in using the appropriate behaviour to achieve his / her goals. Sometimes this means meeting the subordinates expectation, and at other times it may mean confronting them. Faced with someone who is perpetually asking the question, "What should I do about ......?" The expectation from the questioner is an answer, telling them what to do. This satisfies the questioner's current need but does not change anything and the follower will continue to refer similar problems to the leader in future. If the leader's goal is to develop the follower, to enable him or her to make such decisions of their own in future, he / she uses the opportunity presented by the question to lead the follower into making their own decision. This cuts across the expectation and may cause some conflict in the short term, but in the long run the performance of both parties is improved.

Leading your Team

Thus far we have talked about leadership in general terms and how people become leaders because they are seen as satisfying the needs of others. In this chapter we look at needs of people in the workplace and how these can be satisfied by managers thus turning into leaders.

The motivators in the work environment determine the behaviour of people at work. Managers who want motivated employees know they must create the conditions under which people can satisfy their needs in order for them to be motivated to achieve management's goals.

So what is motivation? Motivation can be defined as: The psychological drive to satisfy needs through action

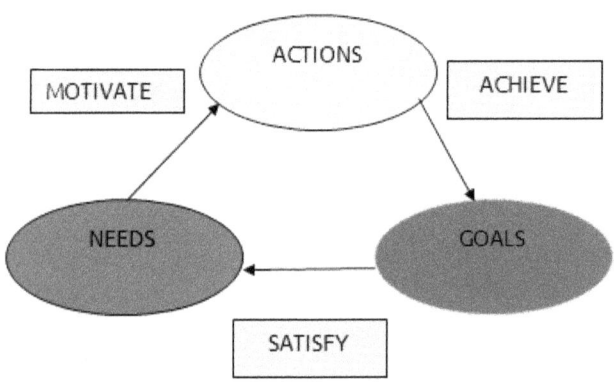

Note. Actions can be both positive and negative. For example; the child who 'needs' recognition will normally start by doing something special to get it. If this fails, it can, in extreme situations lead to the child 'feeding the goldfish to cat' in order to get a response. Just because we are older it does not mean that we are different!

So what motivates people at work? There are many theories of motivation; however it seems to me that the substance of motivation theory is contained in three main pieces of work. Maslow's Hierarchy of Needs, Douglas McGregor's Theory X and Y and Fredrick Herzberg's 'Two Factor Theory'. In 1954 Abraham Maslow suggested that human beings have five different 'sets of needs which they strive to satisfy in ascending order:-

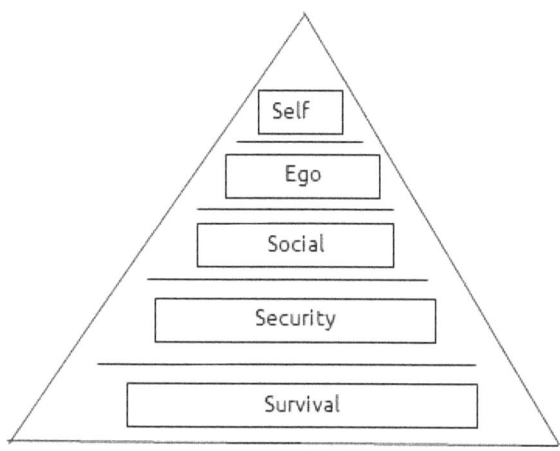

Maslow believed that we move through the various levels of need, depending on the situation in which we find ourselves. The more severe the threat to our survival, the more we are forced to strive to meet our lower level needs. The better the conditions, physically, financially, psychologically, the higher the level of need we strive to satisfy. Thus work, the need to be employed in order to earn money to meet the lower level needs, allows managers to control the behaviour of their employees by simply threatening the employee's security needs. There was historically no need to worry about involvement as a means of motivation; the threat of losing one's job was usually enough to make people conform.

In 1961 Douglas McGregor published his achievement motivation theory. This challenged the traditional view of the working man as someone who needed to be told what to do (Theory X) and postulated the view that man is motivated by the opportunity to achieve (Theory Y). McGregor used examples of what people achieve outside the sterility of the work place demonstrate their innate drive and initiative. Whilst McGregor's work was received with interest in management circles it had little impact in practice. This was primarily because it was not seen as 'practical'.

The third person to impact the work motivation scene was Frederick Herzberg with his Two Factor Theory of Motivation. Herzberg postulated that some things which he called 'motivators' positively motivate people and others, which he called hygiene factors, were neutral when satisfied and de-motivators when not satisfied. He believed that rewarding the motivators and resolving issues connected with the hygiene factors would lead to greater motivation and improved productivity.

Motivators	Hygiene Factors
Achievement Responsibility Worthwhile work Recognition Advancement & growth	Supervision Working conditions Salary Company policy and administration Security

Herzberg's work was embraced with great enthusiasm and led to the birth of the Job Enrichment movement made famous in Europe by such companies as Volvo, British Steel, and British Coal et al. In parallel with this Philips conducted research in one of their TV manufacturing plants into self-managed work groups. Philips took the supervisors out of the groups and made them facilitators. The groups were given the task of organising themselves to produce televisions. The interesting thing about this project was that it revealed that removing the leader, does not remove the need for leadership. The Philips groups developed four natural leaders based on the Charismatic, Personal, Technical and Organisational needs of the group. It was observed that in self-managed work groups different people naturally took these different roles. The 'good speaker' represented the group at meetings; members sought the best 'technician' when they had a technical problem. People with personal problems turned to the 'older and wiser' individual in the group and best organiser organised their affairs.

Unfortunately, with some notable exceptions, most of this work, whilst interesting, produced little real change in organisations. Managers still 'managed' through direction supported economic power and workers continued to 'leave their brains at home'. There is little left now of the Job Enrichment movement or the quality circles so heralded in the 70's. If recent research is to be believed 80% of 'motivational' programmes fail to live up to expectations. Why? There is overwhelming evidence that people like Maslow, McGregor and Herzberg and more recently Deming, Juran and Crosby, are correct in their view that people are achievement motivated, they want to do a good job; they are capable and if only management would let them, will work with their fellows to resolve the organisations problems. So why won't management let them?

The basic problem is managing style. Traditional organisations use a Parent / Child approach to management; one in which power is exercised through the authority to take decisions. Things requiring decisions are pulled to the top of the organisation, instruction flow down. In this way traditional managers maintain their power base and status and are able to satisfy the illusion of control. For the people to be empowered, mangers must give up the detail of decision making. They must accept the right of person doing the job to be involved in deciding the best approach in free association with others and the right to challenge anyone they think is wrong. This means accepting the worker as a partner, someone who has a real contribution to make. Someone who 'brings his/her brains to work' and uses them for the good of the organisation and his/her own personal satisfaction.

The concept of self-managed work teams is clearly feasible, we know it works, and is working in many organisations. We know that people can manage themselves successfully, they do it every day. However introducing such practices means:-

1. changing managing style for parent child to adult
2. devolving power
3. creating the conditions for decision making in the work place
4. developing a climate of trust and respect
5. facilitating the development of all employees
6. recognition that total customer satisfaction is the goal
7. understanding that only output counts

To achieve this management needs to accept that its role is to **harness** the needs of employees so that they are motivated to achieve the organisations goals. This is achieved through involvement supported by appropriate *rewards* and *punishments to* dovetail individual and organisational needs. If people are motivated:-

1. Productivity is high because people who want to do a job put more into it than those who are there under sufferance.
2. Morale is high because people feel involved - they are doing something which they value. This in itself also raises productivity.
3. They work as teams people are working together to achieve organisational goals.

So how can managers harness the needs of their people so that they willingly work to achieve company goals? An enormous amount of research has been carried out into this topic over the years and many interesting and useful theories have been put forward. Most of the work is well covered in any standard textbook on management theory and makes for interesting reading, we however would like to offer the following 'four-factor model' for applying motivational techniques in the workplace.

Using the - The 'Four Factor' Model

The leadership aspect of the manager's role is all about communication. Effective leaders are skilled communicators who empower their people. They work to ensure that their people:

1. know what to do and how to do it
2. feel empowered to be successful
3. understand that help is available to solve the problems they encounter along the way

Achieving this means having a structure which encourages 'motivational communication' between leaders and their teams both at individual and team working levels, Our research shows that in order to be motivated at work people need four types of information from their leaders:-

Task information - They need to know what is expected of them and to receive regular, objective feedback on their performance. Where performance problems are identified they need to be helped to improve.

Personal information - They need the opportunity to meet with their supervisor on a regular basis to discuss the things that concern them like; how am I doing? What does the organisation think about me? What is my future?

Team information - They need the opportunity to meet together with other team members to review performance, learn what is going on and identify and resolve the problems that stop them doing the best job they can.

Company information - They need to meet with and question senior management from time to time to learn directly from them how the organisation is doing and what its future plans are.

Satisfying these needs provides the framework for optimising both performance and job satisfaction; it delineates the leadership aspects of the manager's role. Creating this situation in practice means:

1. Getting Information on where we are now
2. Analysing the results
3. Read the 'meta' message
4. Action - Decide what to do
5. Implement
6. Review and reinforce

Getting Information:

This is done by carrying out a Motivation Survey. This survey indicates how well people's motivational needs are currently being met and highlights areas for improvement. The survey should be completed by all members of the team and if the team leader is responsible for a number of teams, the data should be collated separately to allow for the identification of any specific differences.

MOTIVATION SURVEY

Task Information

1. Are you clear what your job is? Yes / No

2. Do you feel that you have been properly trained for your job? Yes / No

3. Do you have clear performance targets agreed with your supervisor and are you regularly assessed against them? Yes / No

4. Does your supervisor provide help and guidance when you need it? Yes / No

5. Are all the resources, materials, instructions, equipment etc. that you need to do a good job, available to you? Yes / No

Please rate your overall job satisfaction

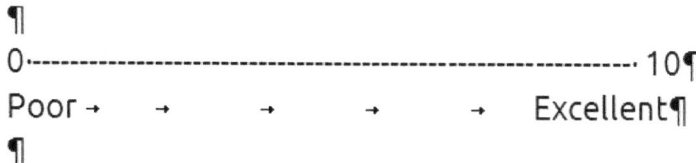

Personal Information

1. Do have regular, i.e. monthly meetings, with your supervisor to discuss how you are doing? Yes / No

2. Do you feel confident that any issues you raise with your supervisor will be dealt with to your satisfaction? Yes / No

3. Do you have a clear idea what the company thinks of you? Yes / No

4. Have you received career guidance from you supervisor? Yes / No

5. Do you have a career development plan which is supported by your supervisor? Yes / No

Please rate your overall satisfaction with the way the company responds to your personal needs.

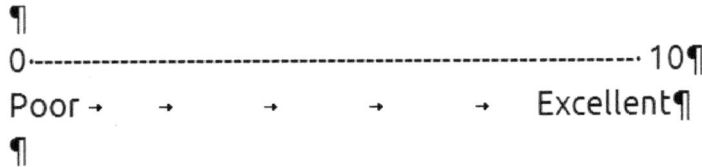

Team Information

1. Do you feel that you understand your team's goals? Yes / No

2. Does your supervisor hold regular weekly/monthly meetings with your team to keep everyone briefed on what is going on, i.e. weekly results, quality etc.? Yes / No

3. Is team working characteristic of the way your Department is managed? Yes / No

4. Do you meet regularly as a team to discuss performance improvement issues such as quality? Yes / No

5. Would you say that openness and trust are characteristic of relationships within your department? Yes / No

Please indicate your current level of satisfaction with your Department.

```
0 ─────────────────────────── 10
Poor  →   →   →   →   →   Excellent
```

Company Information

1. Are you clear what the company's goals are?   Yes / No

2. Does senior management hold regular briefings for all staff setting out the company's past achievements and future objectives?   Yes / No

3. Which of the following media are used to communicate with staff in your company and how effective is it?

	Exists?	Effective?
Senior management briefings	Yes / No	Yes / No
Notice boards	Yes / No	Yes / No
Company newspaper	Yes / No	Yes / No
Quality reports	Yes / No	Yes / No
Senior management 'walkabouts'	Yes / No	Yes / No
Memoranda	Yes / No	Yes / No
Video programmes	Yes / No	Yes / No
Other		

4. Which are most effective the official or the unofficial communication channels?
    Official / Unofficial

5. How interested do you believe senior management to be in hearing your views?
    Very / Not interested

Please indicate your current level of satisfaction on the way the company communicates with you

```
0 ------------------------------------------------- 10
Poor  →     →      →      →       Excellent
```

Please indicate you department – Goods In – Stores – Purchasing – Quality – Test

Analysing the results

Analyse the responses using an Excel spread sheet. The following example is taken from a survey which was carried out at the beginning of a programme to introduce team working into the Maintenance function in one division of a large multi-national company. It was done in order to provide a benchmark against which to assess the effectiveness of the intervention. The findings are set out in four sections as follows:-

    Task Information
    Personal Information
    Team Information
    Company Information

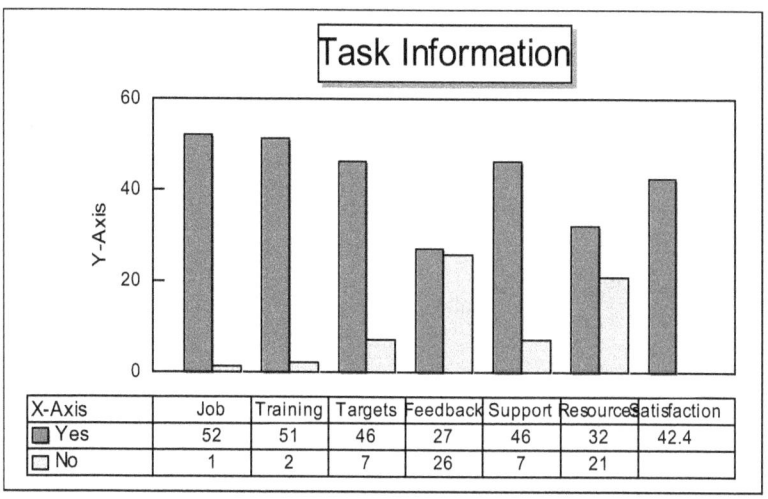

The results indicate that the majority of employees are clear what their job is. They believe they have the training to do the job and are set performance targets. However roughly 50% of respondents do not receive any feedback on whether these targets are achieved. Most feel they have support but 40% say they do not have the resources to do the job well. Respondents express an eighty percent satisfaction rating with their task information

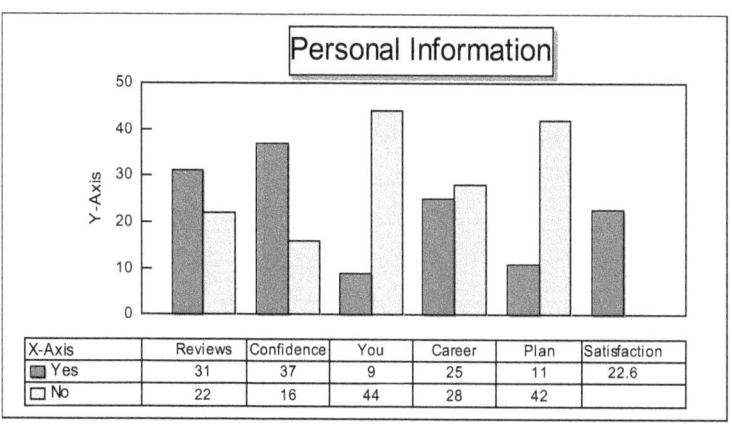

The results indicate that some 40% of respondents do not have regular performance reviews with their supervisors. 33% do not have confidence that their supervisors will deal satisfactorily with problems. 83% do not know what the company thinks about them. Roughly half say they have received career guidance from their supervisor but only eighteen percent say they have a personal development plan. The overall satisfaction rate with personal information is 42%

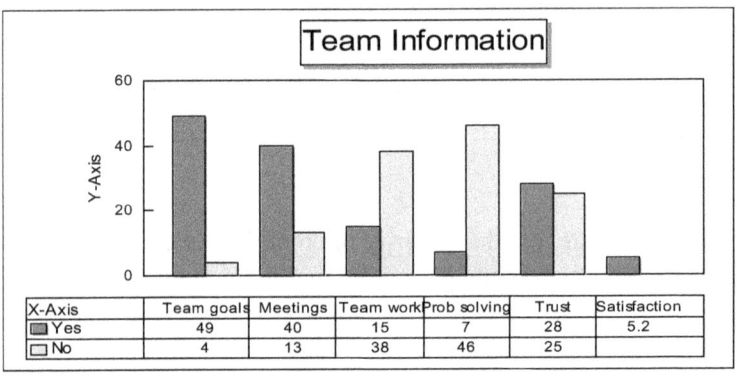

Ninety two percent of respondents believe that they know the goals of their teams and seventy five percent report regular team meetings. However seventy one percent say they are not working as teams and a massive eighty six percent say that they do not work together to solve problems. The views on openness and trust are more or less equally divided; nearly 50% don't trust management. The overall satisfaction level with this information channel is 50%

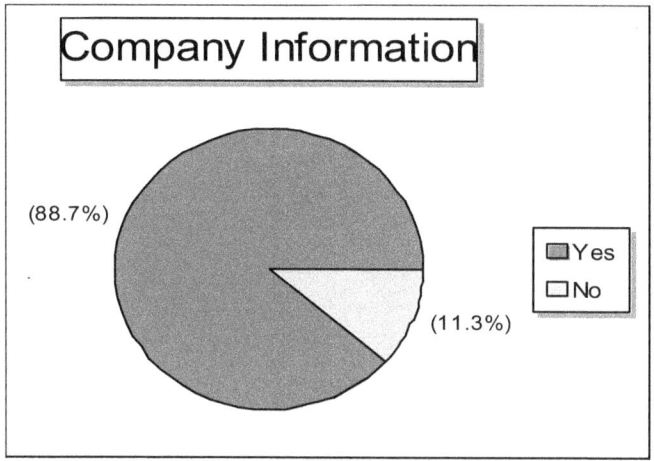

Eighty eight percent indicate that they know what the company's goals are.

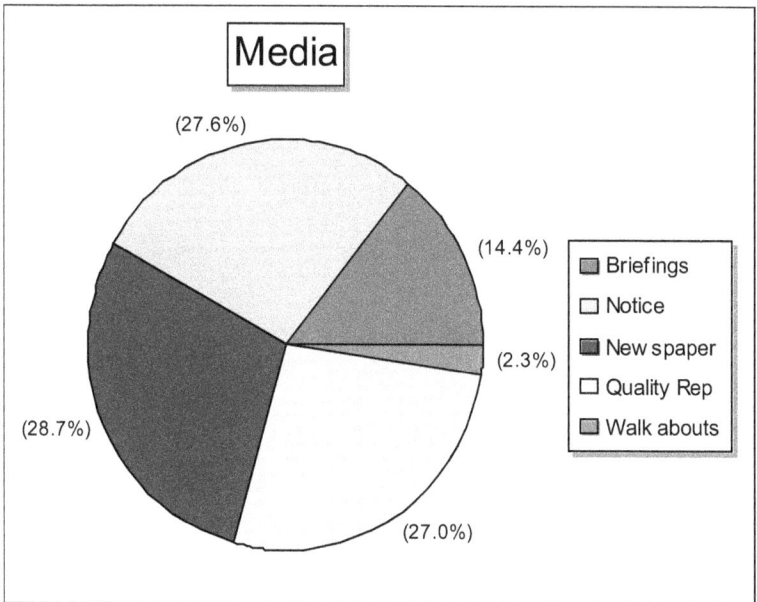

The main tools used to communicate company information are the company newspaper (28%) Notice boards (27%) and Quality reports (27%) Only 14% of information is received through management briefing and only 2% informally   from managers.

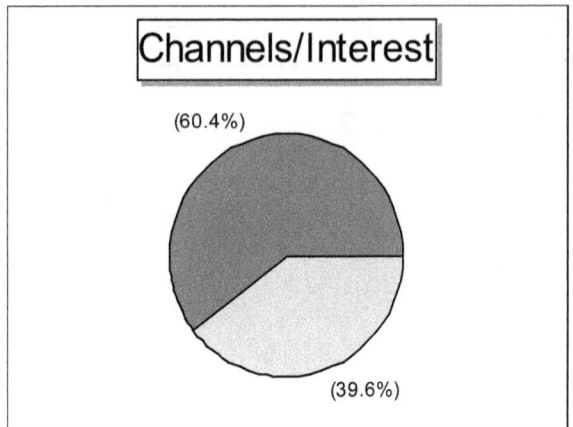

Sixty percent said they find the official channels of communication effective, which means that 40% do not and 54% do not believe that management are interested in their views on things. Only 50% of respondents said that they were satisfied with company information and the way it is communicated. So, what to do?

Read the 'meta' Message

In this case the results show:

The 'majority of employees are satisfied with the 'Task' information they receive; they have the information necessary to do the job.

The main weakness - feedback on achievement

The 'Personal' information results indicate that there is no clear policy on 'personal information' in place. Some people have performance reviews, some don't. Some are satisfied with the way their supervisors handle issues others are not and so on.

The main weakness - inconsistency

The 'Team' information responses indicate that the vast majority know what their team goals are and two thirds do have regular team meetings however this process is clearly more about briefing than team working.

The main weakness – lack of real team working

The 'Company' information responses indicate that the Company is communicating with its people, so they do know what is going on but do not feel involved.

Main weakness - lack of involvement

Action - Decide what to do

So what does this information tell us? Firstly it's important to take into account that this is a survey of a department. This means that there are a number of teams and supervisor involved. Certainly some supervisors will be better leaders than others and we need to keep this in mind when we look at the data.

From the data we can see that this company is doing a good job at communicating 'task needs' to its employees. They know what is expected, they know what is going on but they don't really feel involved; basically because they are not. The leadership style here is 'tell / sell and test' the approach has the 'mechanics of participation' but not the soul. Everyone is working hard and the company is doing well, but they are not working 'smart' management is not 'harnessing' the 'brains' of their people because they are not prepared to share.

If these were the results of a single group we would be able to say that the 'supervisor' needs to be encouraged to be more participative. Under normal circumstances the behaviours required can be empowered by training and ongoing support In this case however we are looking at a 'management' issue. The 'mechanics' of a 'company-wide' communication system are already in place. However if management want to optimise the opportunity offered to harness the 'brains' and energies of their staff they need to introduce a more participative managerial style. This means putting the 'soul' into the procedures which already exist by;

1. changing the structure of the current team meetings from information giving to problem solving
2. encouraging employees to put forward ideas on how to improve performance
3. involving them in finding and implementing solutions

The question is how to do this. If the organisation currently has no participative productivity or continuous improvement programme it's easy, to take one of the 'shelf'. It could be Total Quality Management or 6 Sigma, or GE's Workout programme et al or you can use one of the Japanese programmes, see our book on 'How the Japanese Optimise Productivity'. In this case the company has a robust top down communication structure in place; what it lacks is the element of participation; the involvement of the workforce in a process of **Continuous Improvement** (CI). Our recommendation in this case was that CI should be an integral part of the supervisor's responsibility in the new organisation.

Implement

The recommendations were accepted and we worked with the management team of the division to build a CI component into the existing Performance management system. This required supervisors to encourage their staff to identify issues impacting performance at the weekly production meetings. To create problem solving groups to work on these issues and to run an extend meeting once a month at which project teams report progress In addition the supervisors in each department meet monthly with the departmental manager to report on the achievement of their CI programmes and departmental mangers meet with the Divisional manager the following week to share results. In addition it was agreed to hold quarterly and an annual meeting for all staff in the department to reward performance.

Once the scheme had been agreed a training programme was created to provide the supervisors and departmental manager with the interpersonal and problem solving skills necessary for effective team leadership. When the training phase was complete the Departmental manager held a meeting with all employees to introduce the CI programme.

Review and reinforce

Motivation is a 'fragile flower' that needs to be continually reinforced to maintain momentum. We are very complex beings; constantly being affected by any number of events both inside, and outside work. Motivating people is like maintaining a complex piece of machinery; it requires continual planned maintenance if it is to run at its best. Harnessing employee's drives and dovetailing them with company requirements is not something that can be done just 'once in a while', as with the complex piece of equipment, making frequent, small, adjustments is essential to ensure top performance. It needs to be planned and delivered in a consistent manner by busy managers with very differing personalities who have many competing pressures on their time.

As in the case describe here most organisations have a reward and recognition system as an integral part of the CI process. Regular reviews are also important as is the need to work towards 'best in class'.

In this example the organisation used the 'four factor' model to encourage their supervisors to become team leaders and through this to optimise performance. Reward and recognition are the key to a motivated workforce, how you do it depends on what is right for you.

The Way Ahead

People follow those who they believe:

> *Know where they are going*
> *Know how to get there*
> *Have the courage to travel*

Do people follow you? If you would like to find we suggest you start the process by assessing your current leadership profile. The following questionnaire is designed to help you do this.

Leadership Skills – Self Assessment Check List

Process

My manager provides me with the team goals which I communicate to them, we then discus to agree how we will meet them.

☐ Good   ☐ Satisfactory   ☐ Need Improvement

I agree roles and responsibilities with team members

☐ Good   ☐ Satisfactory   ☐ Need Improvement

We have procedures in place for measuring results

☐ Good   ☐ Satisfactory   ☐ Need Improvement

We have regular performance review meetings; where we identify issues we discuss to agree appropriate actions

☐ Good   ☐ Satisfactory   ☐ Need Improvement

I am responsible for reviewing the performance of my team and providing them with objective positive and when necessary, corrective feedback

☐ Good   ☐ Satisfactory   ☐ Need Improvement

I provide coaching support to help team members develop new skills and counselling help where necessary

☐ Good   ☐ Satisfactory   ☐ Need Improvement

I am responsible the quality of the work dione by the team and for ensuring that standard procedures are adhered to.

☐ Good   ☐ Satisfactory   ☐ Need Improvement

I am responsible for the Health & Safety of the team

☐ Good   ☐ Satisfactory   ☐ Need Improvement

I see continuous improvement as a key aspect of my roll and work with the team to achieve specific outcomes

☐ Good   ☐ Satisfactory   ☐ Need Improvement

Skills

I am able to develop and maintain rapport through matching non-verbal behaviour

☐ Good   ☐ Satisfactory   ☐ Need Improvement

I understand what motivates my team and take this into account when making decisions

☐ Good ☐ Satisfactory ☐ Need Improvement

I am flexible and able to use the most appropriate leadership style for the situation

☐ Good ☐ Satisfactory ☐ Need Improvement

I am prepared and able to negotiate win / won solutions based on workable compromise

☐ Good ☐ Satisfactory ☐ Need Improvement

I am able to make compelling presentations

☐ Good ☐ Satisfactory ☐ Need Improvement

I am able to manage meetings and offer appropriate process models for solving specific problems

☐ Good ☐ Satisfactory ☐ Need Improvement

I am able to use assertive behaviours in order to defuse conflict

☐ Good ☐ Satisfactory ☐ Need Improvement

I recognise that I am not perfect and seek regular feedback both from the team and others we interact with in order to improve my performance

☐ Good ☐ Satisfactory ☐ Need Improvement

Having completed the questionnaire you can now identify those things that you feel you do well and those where you can improve. However, before you 'rush' of to HR to seek some training we suggest that you find someone who knows you well and using the statements in this questionnaire as questions ask them how they see you.. If you are really open about your relationships you could ask your team for feedback!

Once you are clear what you need to do to become a more effective leader you need to take action. Weaknesses in the process area are relatively easy to do something about. If for example you can, as in the case study look for and implement a 'packaged' solution. However if you need to improve your Meetings management Skills, we would suggest a short training course followed by a period of supported practice and so on.

We hope you have found the book interesting and that it will motivate you to develop your leadership skills.

Bon chance et bon courage

George Boulden, April 2015

Further Reading

If you have found reading this book interesting you may you may also find the following useful.

1. For an insight into human behaviour I recommend Dr. Thomas A. Harris is the author of *I'm OK – You're OK*, the 1969 bestseller based upon the ideas of Transactional Analysis by Dr Eric Berne. ISBN 0-06-072427. If you find this interesting you may also like to read 'The Games People Play, by Dr Eric Berne ISBN 0-345-41003-3

2. In the same géndre but more focused on 'rapport' skills is NPL, How to Build a Successful Life by Richard Brandler, Alessio Roberti & Owen Fitzpatrick, published by Harper Collins, ISBN 978-0-00-749741-6

3. For a deeper understanding of values I suggest 'What Matters Most' by Hyrum W Smith, published by Franklin Covey Co. ISBN 0-684-87256-0

4. For an entertaining insight into the real world of influencing I recommend the book 'When I Stop Talking You'll Know I'm Dead by Jerry Weintraub, Rich Cohen and George Clooney, Published by Hachette Books ISBN 978-0-446-54815-1

5. To learn more about 'action learning' I recommend Reg's original book on the subject 'The ABC of Action Learning' Published by Gower Publications, ISBN 978-1-4094-2703-2 Mike Pedlars Action Learning in Practice, Third Edition, Ed Mike Pedler, Gower Press, ISBN 0 566 07795 7 and More than Management Development, Edited by David Casey & David Pearce, Gower Press, 1977. ISBN 0-566-022005-X This book reviews the early GEC programmes referred to in this text.

6. If you would like to learn more about Facilitation then 'Facilitating Action Learning: A Practitioner's Guide' by Mike Pedler and Christine Abbott is a useful read. Also David Casey's excellent paper on The Emerging Role of the Set Advisers, copies available from ALA International

Books George has written on Action Learning and related topics

The following books are published by ALA International. they are available on our web site www.ala-international.com and from **Google Books** and **Amazon** in Epub or paperback formats.

Books about Action learning

Applications of Action Learning – describes the philosophy of action learning and its applications. ISBN 978-0-9560822-4-4

In-Plant Action Learning – explains how the philosophy of Action learning can be used to deliver organisational change. ISBN 978-0-9560822-3-7

In-Plant Action Learning Teams, Participants Guide – This Guide is designed to help In-Plant teams to self-manage and facilitate their own learning; available from ALA International.

Facilitated Learning – describes facilitation as applied in Action Learning programmes. ISBN 978-0 -9560822-9-9

Books about Personal Development

Managers as Leaders - This book show how management and leadership combine to ensure the effective delivery of the task. ISBN 978-0-9560822-2-0

Managing Difficult Relationships – examines the reasons for difficult relationships and provides a 'framework' for negotiating win / win solutions. ISBN 978-0-9560822-5-1

Change; Become a Winner - I believe that life is not a rehearsal, it's a journey and you can change it. If you would like to do something different with your life this book is for you. ISBN 13 978-1503185401, ISBN 10:1503185400

Re-Engineering the Workplace – describes the Japanese approach to productivity

Useful web sites

Action Learning is a worldwide network. The following are some useful contacts in the Action Learning world:-

The International Foundation for Action Learning (IFAL), formally The Action Learning Trust www.ifal.org.uk

International Community of Action Learners (ICAL) This is a loose federation of Action Learning practitioners. Their web site can be found on www.tlainc.com

IMC acts as a clearing house for academic institutions offering Action Learning programmes. Contact www.imc.org.uk/imcal-inter For articles www.free-press.com/journals/gaja

The Revan's Library at Salford University www.salford.ac.uk

World Institute for Action Learning, www.wial.com

www.ingramcontent.com/pod-product-compliance
Lightning Source LLC
Chambersburg PA
CBHW061345040426
42444CB00011B/3094